LUNG CANCER

LUNG CANCER

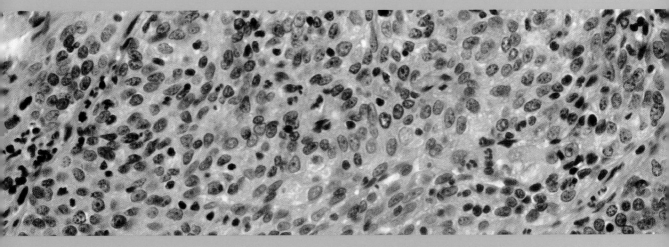

Marlene Targ Brill

BENCHMARK BOOKS

MARSHALL CAVENDISH
NEW YORK

For Mom, who bore the difficult struggle with
her usual strength, dignity, and humor.

With thanks to Renato N. Mascardo, M.D., FACE, FACP, Assistant Clinical Professor of Medicine, Division of Endocrinology & Metabolism, University of Connecticut School of Medicine, for his expert review of the manuscript.

Benchmark Books
Marshall Cavendish
99 White Plains Road
Tarrytown, New York 10591-9001
www.marshallcavendish.com

Library of Congress Cataloging-in-Publication Data
Brill, Marlene Targ.
    Lung cancer / Marlene Targ Brill.
      p. cm. — (Health alert)
  Includes bibliographical references and index.
    ISBN 0-7614-1802-4
  1. Lungs Cancer—Juvenile literature. I. Title. II. Series: Health alert (Benchmark Books).
    RC280.L8B75 2005
    616.99'424—dc22

                              2004005971

Front cover: A chest X ray that shows a lung tumor (bottom left, in red)
Title page: A microscopic sample of small cell lung cancer

Photo research by Regina Flanagan

Front cover: Du Cane Medical Imaging Ltd / Photo Researchers, Inc.

The photographs in this book are used by permission and through the courtesy of: *Photo Researchers, Inc.:* CNRI, 3, 18; Joubert, 5, 28; SPL, 9, 15, 35; Bo Veisland, Mi & I, 11 (top); Alfred Pasieka, 11 (bottom); John Bavosi, 12; Moredun Scientific, 13; S. Fraser, 14; Du Cane Medical Imaging Ltd., 16; VEM, 17; Dr. E. Walker, 19; St. Bartholomew's Hospital, 24; National Cancer Institute, 27; David Gifford, 31; Kings College School of Medicine, 33, (Department of Surgery) 37; National Library of Medicine, 34; Sheila Terry, 36; Jean–Paul Chassenet, 41; Simon Fraser, 45; Volker Steger, 46; Garo, 47; Stevie Grand, 51; Sam Ogden, 52. *Corbis:* Hulton-Deutsch Collection, 38; Bettmann, 39; Najlah Feanny, 43. *PictureQuest:* Jonathan A. Meyers / Stock Connection, 21; Garo Phanie, Rex Interstock / Stock Connection, 29.

Printed in China

6 5 4 3 2 1

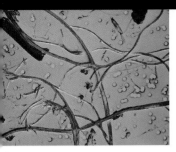

CONTENTS

Chapter 1   What Is Life Like with Lung Cancer?   6

Chapter 2   What is Lung Cancer?   8

Chapter 3   The History of Cancer   32

Chapter 4   Diagnosing, Treating, and Coping

with Lung Cancer   42

Glossary   58

Find Out More   60

Index   63

WHAT IS LIFE LIKE WITH LUNG CANCER?

Kate loved her grandmother, but she hated that her grandmother smoked. Kate was worried that smoking was harming her grandmother's health. Grandma coughed constantly. All of the coughing made Grandma's voice raspy. The coughing interrupted their conversations and interfered with their other fun activities together.

Over time, the coughs became worse. The sound deepened, and the waves of coughing lasted longer, sometimes for many minutes without stopping. Besides the cough, Grandma suffered a steady stream of colds and flu. She **wheezed** during the day and snored at night. When Grandma breathed, Kate thought it sounded like an old engine that was breaking down. If Grandma moved too quickly or walked too far, she could not catch her breath. On one walk with Kate, Grandma became so short of breath that she had to rest against a parking meter.

Soon Grandma started experiencing other health problems. She developed a fever. A light touch on her arm would cause a lot of pain.

Shoulder pain also kept her up at night. Grandma felt so tired that it took her a long time just to get out of bed every morning.

With each new problem, Grandma went to her doctor. The doctor gave her medicine for the colds and flu. He said the pains and tiredness were normal for someone who was seventy-seven years old. Grandma eventually went to another doctor who treated breathing problems. After running some tests, this doctor determined that Grandma's breathing problems stemmed from lung cancer. The other pains and health problems came from cancer that had spread from her lungs to other parts of her body. Grandma, Kate, and the rest of their family were stunned and scared. They were very worried about Grandma's future.

After finding out she had cancer, Grandma saw another doctor who focused on cancer. These doctors are called oncologists. The oncologist told Grandma that she needed to stop smoking. He gave her vitamins and told her to eat healthful foods. She was also supposed to exercise as best she could. The medical treatment for cancer included surgery to remove body tissue that had cancer. Grandma also had **radiation** treatments and **chemotherapy**. These procedures are supposed to stop the cancer cells from growing and spreading.

The treatments were difficult for Grandma. Some were painful and made her very weak. But she was lucky that she had the support of Kate and the rest of her family. Their constant care and encouragement helped Grandma through the cancer treatments.

WHAT IS LUNG CANCER?

Cancer is an illness that begins in the cells of the body. Cells are the smallest unit of any living thing. The body contains millions of cells. Cells are responsible for everything that occurs in the body. Organs and other body parts are made up of different cells. Most healthy cells are able to grow and multiply to form new cells.

Cancer cells are damaged or **abnormal**. This means that something is wrong with them and they do not behave like normal healthy cells. Usually, damaged cells repair themselves or they die. Cancer cells, however, multiply quickly, creating more cells with **defects**. Soon this growth gets out of control. The defective cells invade or interfere with healthy cells. This upsets normal body functions, making a person sick.

There are many different types of cancers. Cancer types are determined by which organs or body systems are affected. Different cancers may occur in the lungs, breast, stomach, or

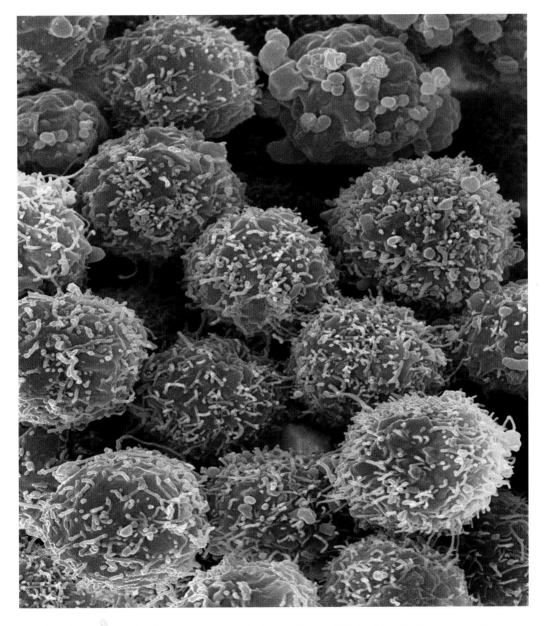

A colored scanning electron micrograph (a type of magnified picture) shows many lung cancer cells clumped together.

Tumors

....

When cells multiply too rapidly they can clump together to form abnormal growths. These growths are called masses or **tumors.** Tumors may bulge out from the body. When this happens, the tumors can usually be felt by touch. But not all tumors can be felt. As is often the case with lung cancer, the tumors are located deep inside the body. Doctors need to use X rays or other machines to see the tumors.

Sometimes tumors are **benign**, or harmless. Problems occur when tumors are **malignant**, or made up of cancer cells. Not every form of cancer causes tumors. For example, breast cancer patients usually suffer from malignant tumors, but leukemia patients, however, do not.

blood, which is called leukemia. Each type of cancer has different **symptoms** (signs of sickness), growth rates, and treatments. In order to understand lung cancer, one must first have an idea of how the lungs function.

THE LUNGS

The lungs are part of the **respiratory system**, the set of body parts that move air into and out of the body. Most people are born with a right lung and a left lung. The left lung has two sections, or lobes. The right lung has three lobes. The left lung is smaller to make room for the heart, which lies slightly to the left between the two lobes of the left lung. Around the lungs is a covering called pleura. This slippery tissue separates the lobes and protects them as they move during breathing.

Air comes in through the nose or mouth. Incoming air contains oxygen, a gas that fuels blood cells. The air travels through the windpipe, or trachea, into the lungs. Lungs contain a complex system of airways that looks like an upside-down tree. From the trachea, air goes into smaller tubelike branches in the lungs called bronchi. (Each of the bronchi is called a bronchus.) The bronchi divide into even smaller branches called bronchioles.

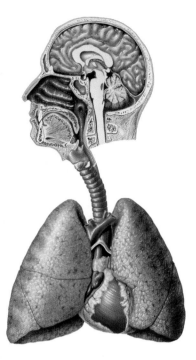

Parts of the respiratory system include the trachea (shown in blue) and the right and left lungs.

The ends of bronchioles contain alveoli, millions of tiny air sacs that expand as air fills them. Healthy lungs have more than 300 million alveoli. If all of a person's alveoli were cut, flattened, and laid side to side, their surface would almost equal the size of a tennis court. Surrounding the alveoli are tiny blood vessels called

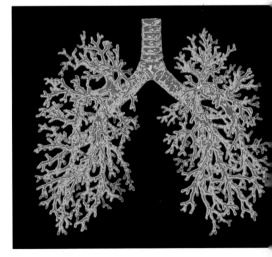

A computer image shows how the bronchi branch into many tiny bronchioles.

capillaries. Oxygen from the alveoli is transferred to the blood in the capillaries. The blood with oxygen is then transported to cells throughout the body.

After cells use oxygen, they produce a gas called carbon dioxide. For humans, carbon dioxide gas inside the body is a waste material and should be exhaled. The blood in the capillaries around the alveoli transfers carbon dioxide to the alveoli. From there, the carbon

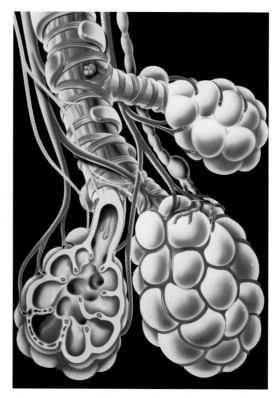

The walls of the alveoli are very thin. This makes it easier for gases to be exchanged between capillaries and the alveoli.

dioxide travels back up through the bronchioles and bronchi, and is then released through the mouth or nose.

CANCER IN THE LUNGS

Tumors from lung cancer can grow anywhere in the respiratory system, though most lung cancers originate in the bronchi. As tumors grow, they can affect normal lung function, reducing or cutting off the oxygen supply. This leaves the rest of the body without enough oxygen to work properly. The body becomes weak and tired, and it takes more effort to carry out normal activities. As a result, a person becomes short of breath. Difficulty with inhaling enough air and breathing too quickly are two of the more common signs of lung cancer.

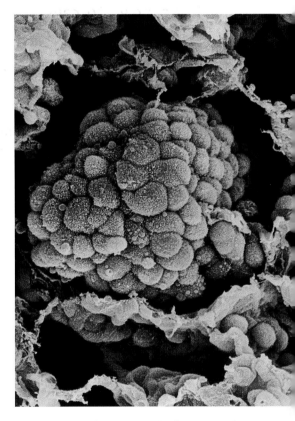

Tumors also steal nutrients from healthy cells in the lungs. As large tumors grow, they take up more space, damaging or killing healthy tissue. The larger the tumor, the more problems it causes. Since lungs have a lot of space inside, tumors can grow for some time before causing enough trouble to be detected.

Sometimes tumors block the normal flow of fluids in and out of the lungs. **Mucus** is an example of a lung fluid that is affected by tumors. Mucus is a sticky liquid that is found on the walls of the airways.

Cancer cells (shown in pink) are growing among alveolar sacs (shown in brown, white, and yellow) in the lungs.

It keeps the airways moist and filters the inhaled air by trapping dust and other particles. Tiny hairlike structures called **cilia** line the airways and also filter inhaled air. Mucus is usually

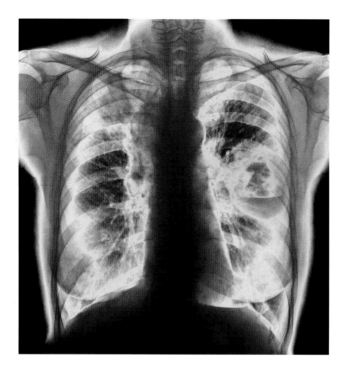

The yellow structure in this colored X ray is a tumor made up of lung cancer cells.

swallowed or sneezed or coughed out. Lung tumors can prevent mucus from leaving the lungs. The buildup of mucus (and the particles it is trying to filter) contributes to an increased number of colds, flu, and serious lung infections. Extra mucus also contributes to different breathing sounds. Lung cancer may cause wheezing, grunting, or talking with a raspy voice because extra fluid blocks the airways.

People with lung cancer may cough a lot to get rid of built-up mucus. (Healthy people also cough, so coughing is not necessarily a sign of lung cancer.) Coughing can be painful for people with lung cancer. They might cough up more mucus than usual. They might also cough up blood.

Some tumors release substances into the bloodstream. These substances can cause a loss of appetite and weight

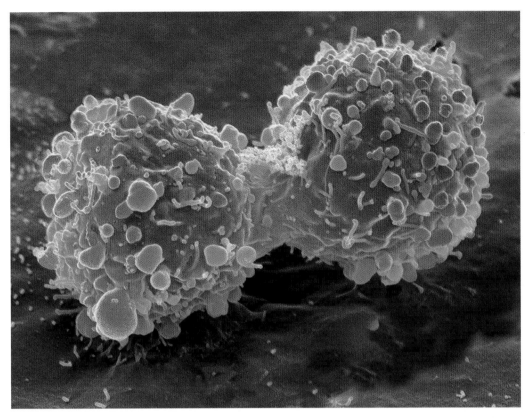

Many lung cancer cells can reproduce and spread quickly, forming large tumors throughout the lungs.

loss. They can also interfere with the blood supply to and from the lungs. The buildup of extra blood could produce swelling in the face or neck.

Tumors may also cause other unusual aches and pains, depending upon where they grow. Throughout the body, a network of **nerves** sends signals to the brain, causing feelings such as coldness, warmth, itchiness, or pain. Tumors that grow in different parts of the respiratory system may press on nerves, causing back, chest, shoulder, or arm pain.

Sometimes cancer that starts in the lungs spreads to other parts of the body. **Metastasis** occurs when cancer cells from one organ spread to another organ or body system. The cancer cells travel through the bloodstream to other parts of the body, causing many problems. New tumors can grow from

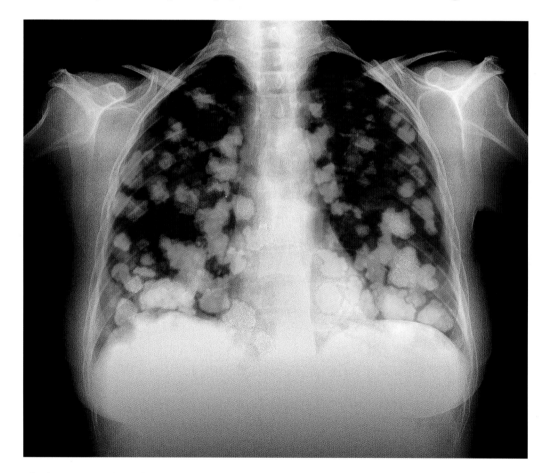

The lung cancer in this patient has metastasized throughout the lungs. The orange spots in this X ray represent multiple tumors.

The Lymphatic System

....

The human lymphatic system is a complex network of vessels located throughout the body. Lymphatic vessels transport and remove different fluids to and from parts of the body. The lymphatic system also plays an important part in fighting infection. Lymphocytes are special infection-fighting white blood cells found in the lymph nodes. Lymph nodes are small tissue masses located along the different lymphatic vessels. These bean-shaped nodes help to filter harmful substances.

Cancer, however, often takes advantage of the lymph nodes and the efficient lymphatic system. When cancer metastasizes, the cancerous cells can move from organs into nearby lymph nodes. The cancer takes over the nodes and spreads more cancer cells by using the vessels of the lymphatic system. Many lymph nodes are located in the upper body, especially near the armpits and neck. If cancer is suspected, doctors can remove a lymph node and test it. From this, the doctor may be able to determine how far the cancer has spread. Lymph nodes with cancerous growths are usually removed through surgery.

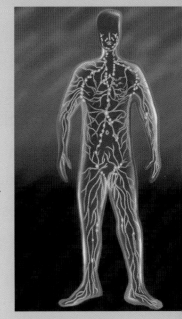

The orange lines in this illustration represent the network of lymphatic vessels. Lymph nodes are shown as yellow circles.

these scattered cancer cells. Metastasis can spread quickly, or it can happen over a long period of time.

Unfortunately, cancer that has metastasized to multiple organs is usually deadly. Organ systems fail, the body cannot function, and the patient eventually dies.

TYPES OF LUNG CANCER

Doctors talk about two main kinds of lung cancer: small cell lung cancer and non-small cell lung cancer. Each involves cells that look different under a **microscope**. The names reflect the shape rather than size of the tumors. So far, doctors have discovered many different types of cancer within these two groups.

Small cell lung cancer. This type of cancer is sometimes called oat cell cancer because the cancer cells look like oats. Small cell cancer usually develops in the bronchi. With this kind of cancer, the cells form large tumors that spread quickly.

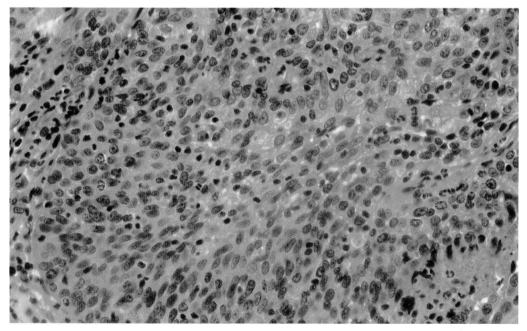

A magnified image shows a tissue sample from the lungs of a person with small cell lung cancer.

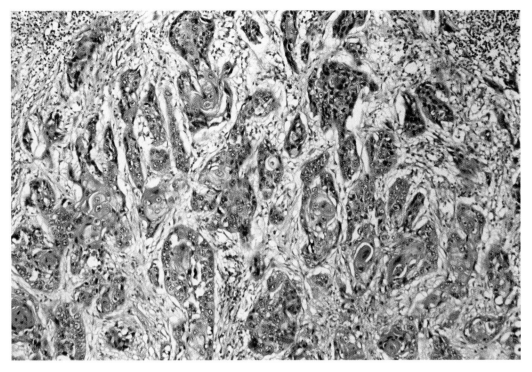

Cells of non-small cell lung cancer are shaped differently from small cell cancer cells.

Small-cell tumors double their size within thirty days. About one in four cancers come from small cells. Almost all small cell cancers are caused by smoking.

Non-small cell lung cancer. This type of lung cancer is more common, and accounts for about eight out of ten cases. Tumors of non-small cells grow slower than small-cell tumors. These tumors take up to six months to double in size. Most often, non-small cancer stays contained in one tumor without spreading to other parts of the lungs and body. Different non-small cells form in smaller airways. They are linked with smoking but can form in nonsmokers as well.

Treatments vary, depending upon the type of cancer. It is important to discover the type of cancer someone has, where tumors are, and where they came from. Only then can doctors make a treatment plan.

WHAT CAUSES LUNG CANCER?

No one knows for sure why some people develop lung cancer while others do not. But scientists and health professionals do know that lung cancer is not contagious like a cold or flu virus. You cannot "catch" lung cancer from someone who has it. To determine the cause of lung cancer, doctors look at a patient's smoking history, possible exposure to cancer-causing substances, and family medical history.

Smoking

When a person smokes, he or she inhales chemicals and other substances from the tobacco product. These substances damage the alveoli. The damaged alveoli have difficulty transferring oxygen from the lungs to the blood. The blood that circulates throughout the body ends up having less oxygen. Without oxygen from the blood, many cells cannot function properly and die. As a result, a person starts to develop health problems.

According to laws in the United States, tobacco companies are required to include warning labels on tobacco products. These labels point out the health risks linked to using cigarettes, cigars, or smokeless tobacco.

Cells that are repeatedly exposed to these chemicals can change to become cancer cells.

The American Lung Association claims that about 87 percent of lung cancers come from smoking tobacco. This makes smoking the leading cause of lung cancer. Studies show that states with the highest smoking rates report the most deaths from lung cancer.

More than half of the lung cancer cases in the United States today occur in men, but an alarming trend involves the increased rates of lung cancer found in women. Seventy years ago, lung cancer in women was rare. At the time, few girls or women were smoking. More women started to smoke in the 1940s. Twenty years later, the numbers of lung cancer deaths in women skyrocketed. By 1987, lung cancer was the leading cause of cancer deaths in women.

Recent studies show that women seem more likely to be affected by smoking than men. Women who become **addicted** to smoking find it harder to quit than men. In addition, scientists found that anti-smoking gum and patches are less effective on women than on men. As a result, women are two times more likely than men to suffer lung cancer and other smoking-related illnesses, such as heart disease and stroke. These statistics have convinced lung cancer researchers to examine the many biological and **genetic** differences between men and women. By investigating these differences, scientists might someday find out what role these things play in developing—and treating—lung cancer.

The longer someone smokes, the greater chance he or she has of developing lung cancer. Quitting smoking can help to reduce that chance, but people who once smoked and then stopped are still at greater risk of developing lung cancer than those who never smoked. But the body has an amazing ability to heal itself. Long periods of not smoking can increase the chance that healthy cells will replace unhealthy ones. If smokers develop lung cancer

Smoking Facts

....

• Smoke from tobacco products such as cigarettes, pipes, and cigars consists of more than 4,000 different ingredients. Some of these ingredients are also found in rat poison, paint stripper, rocket fuel, lighter fluid, mothballs, and antifreeze. So far, more than forty of these ingredients have been proven to produce cancer.

• Today, 4.5 million teenagers smoke. Of those who continue to smoke, at least one million can expect to die from lung cancer by the time they reach their sixties.

• Pets that live in smoke-filled homes are at greater risk of developing infections that lead to cancer. One scientific study claims that cats living in homes in which one or more packs of cigarettes are smoked each day are three times more likely to develop cancer than cats that live in smoke-free environments.

• Non-smokers who are married to smokers are thirty times more likely to develop lung cancer than those who are married to non-smokers.

• According to one study, parents who smoke admit that **secondhand smoke** can be harmful, yet less than one in five ban smoking in their homes.

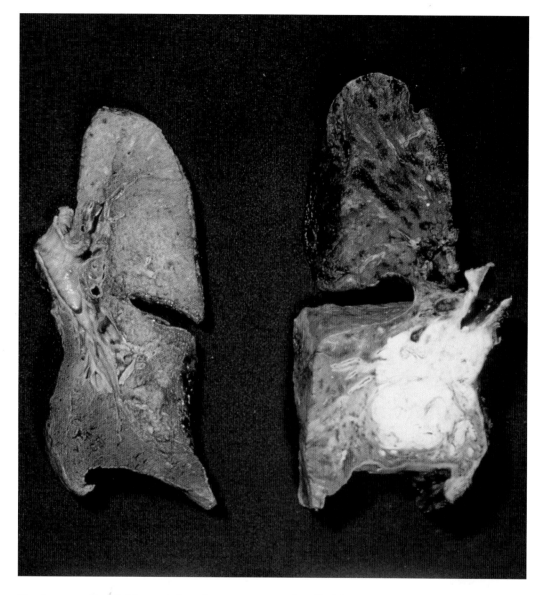

The lung on the right was taken from someone who died from lung cancer. The white mass at the bottom is a tumor and the lung tissue was damaged and blackened from long-term smoking. By comparison, the lung shown on the left is from a healthy person who did not smoke.

and then stop smoking, they reduce the chance that lung cancer will return after treatment. Some people find it difficult to give up smoking, so they join programs offered to help people stop. Smokers who want to quit can get a lot of information and support from online groups. The American Lung Association offers a 24-hour support hotline (1-800-LUNG-USA) for people who are interested in quitting.

Studies have shown that people can develop lung cancer and other health problems from secondhand smoke. Secondhand smoke is smoke from a smoker that is inhaled by others. People who spend a lot of time in smoky areas increase their chances of developing lung cancer. Secondhand smoke accounts for about 3,000 deaths from lung cancer each year.

Family Medical History

People whose parents, sisters, or brothers had lung cancer are at greater risk of getting the disease. Part of the risk comes from sharing the same environment. A household with smokers can damage anyone's lungs. Another risk involves passing the disease from parent to child through genes. Genes are the tiny parts of cells that determine features and characteristics from hair color to the potential to develop certain diseases. A child inherits these genes from either or both parents. This is how certain diseases or the likelihood of developing diseases are passed on in families.

Oncogenes are genes that cause cancer. Researchers also believe that something in the environment interacts with one or more genes to trigger tumor growth in the lungs. So far, two genes have been linked to lung cancer. However, a person is not necessarily going to develop cancer just because some genes they have inherited from their parents can cause cancer.

Poisons in the Air

One in six new lung cancer patients have never smoked. Besides secondhand smoke, these people may be breathing in other air pollutants, which then cause lung cancer. Scientists and health professionals have identified and continue to discover many substances that cause lung cancer. These cancer-causing agents are called **carcinogens.**

Radon. Radon is a colorless, odorless gas that is found in soil and rocks. The gas often seeps into houses and buildings through cracks in the walls or building foundation or through pipes and drains. Inhaling radon damages the lungs and can lead to lung cancer. The National Cancer Institute links radon exposure to 15,000 to 22,000 lung cancer deaths each year.

Radon monitors can be used to test the radon levels in homes and other buildings.

Miners who work below ground where the gas is plentiful have the greatest risk of radon-induced lung cancer. One in fifteen homes in the United States has radon levels that are too high. To protect people, schools and workplaces must maintain safe radon levels. The government has determined what the safe levels of radon should be.

Asbestos. This mineral was used to make supplies used for manufacturing, building materials, and electrical supplies. In the 1970s, however, most companies stopped using asbestos in their products. Scientists had discovered that tiny asbestos fibers entered the air and were then inhaled by people who spent time around material made with asbestos. The inhaled asbestos interfered with normal lung function and lung cancer often developed in the pleura. Besides causing lung cancer, long term exposure to asbestos often resulted in a lung disease

A magnified view of asbestos fibers. Over time and in large amounts, these fibers can cause serious lung damage.

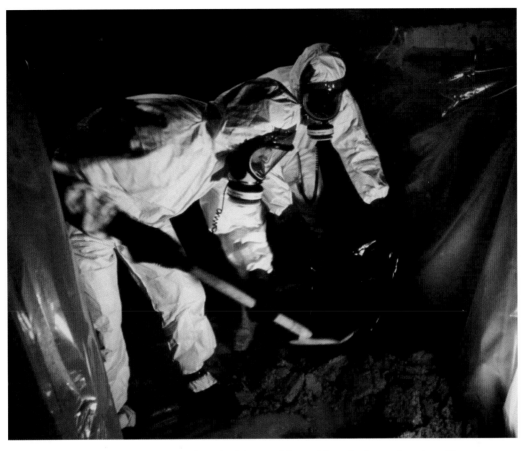

Workers must use special protective clothing and breathing devices when handling asbestos.

called asbestosis. People who suffered from asbestosis had difficulty breathing and had damaged lungs.

Federal and state governments have banned the use of asbestos in most home and workplace products. Older buildings may still contain wallboard, floor tile, or other products composed of asbestos. Most of these products pose

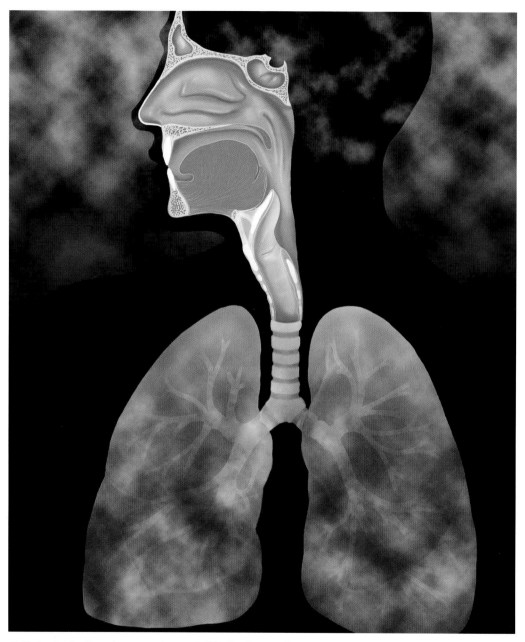

Pollutants in the air can enter and fill the lungs. Frequent exposure to air pollutants can damage lung tissue.

no harm unless they fall apart and release asbestos dust. To prevent any future problems, many schools and government buildings have replaced asbestos building materials with newer asbestos-free products. Unfortunately, the government has not yet addressed limits on many other products that contain asbestos. Workers who handle brake linings, filters, and fireproof materials might be at a high risk of developing lung cancer from the asbestos in these products.

Air Pollutants. There are other carcinogens that are dangerous, and many of them cannot be avoided. People who work with or live near uranium, arsenic, talc, vinyl chloride, nickel chromates, coal, mustard gas, ethers, gasoline, and diesel fuel may develop lung cancer. These people should use safety precautions when handling the materials and carefully monitor their health.

In the United States, doctors find more than 169,400 new cases of lung cancer each year. Lung cancer claims about 157,200 lives a year and is the second leading cause of death in the United States. In a few cases, lung cancer is not preventable. But by choosing a healthy lifestyle and understanding—and avoiding—the potential causes of lung cancer, most people can reduce their chances of developing this disease.

3

THE HISTORY OF CANCER

Many historians believe that physicians knew about cancer (though it was not called *cancer*) thousands of years ago. Ancient Egyptian records showed that physicians from around 2500 to 1600 B.C.E. were able to identify tumors. They performed surgery to remove some tumors but also applied medicine and magic to try to treat the disease. Scientists even found ancient mummies and other human skeletal remains with signs of cancer.

The Greek physician Hippocrates (460 to 370 B.C.E.), who is often called the Father of Medicine, made many medical contributions to understanding and treating cancer and other illnesses. Some historians claim that Hippocrates was the first physician to sort benign tumors from malignant tumors. He is also credited with using the words *carcinoma* and *carcinos* to describe different types of tumors. These words come from

The Erb's papyrus is an ancient Egyptian document that includes descriptions of breast cancer.

Hippocrates was a well-respected physician who taught many students. He was one of the first physicians to believe that diseases were caused by physical problems and not by the gods.

the Greek word for crab. Hippocrates probably felt that the structure of tumors—specifically the way parts of the tumors branch out—resembled a crab. Today the word carcinoma is used to describe the most common type of cancer.

From Hippocrates's time to the nineteenth century, scientists made several discoveries about the human body and the illnesses that affected it. Identifying cancer became more common. But because scientists still did not know enough about how the body works, no one really knew what caused cancer and how the disease spread.

A lack of technology like we have today made it difficult to prevent or treat cancer. The invention of the compound microscope in the 1500s helped physicians learn more about the

Scientists and physicians learned a lot about the human body through dissection. They cut into the body to examine it. This illustration shows a sixteenth-century dissection class.

body and its cells. Now they could see healthy and unhealthy tissues and cells. The invention of the microscope did not lead directly to a clearer understanding of cancer, but such advances led to more discoveries about the human body. For example, in the seventeenth century, the scientist Gaspare Aselli discovered the human lymphatic system. By testing and observing the vessels and the lymph, Aselli thought that cancer was caused by an abnormal lymphatic system.

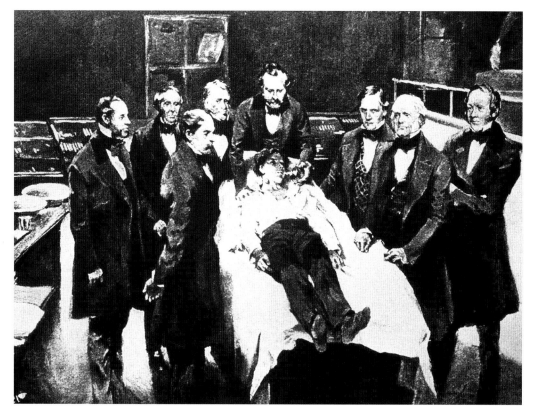

A painting illustrates the first public demonstration of surgical anesthesia. This surgery was performed in 1846 at the Massachusetts General Hospital.

Later improvements in surgical techniques helped cancer patients and their physicians. As doctors used cleaner surgery methods, more patients survived after having tumors removed. Anesthesia—which numbs a person or puts him or her to sleep during medical procedures—also proved helpful. Doctors could take more time to remove large or far-reaching cancer growths. Cancer patients had higher survival rates. Knowing that anesthesia would be used during surgery convinced more cancer patients to have surgery.

THE NINETEENTH AND TWENTIETH CENTURIES

Progress in scientific discoveries lead to better cancer **diagnosis** and treatment. Around the 1890s, scientists gained a better understanding of radiation and how energy can be released in waves and particles. Soon after X-ray machines were developed. Physicians used X rays to see inside a person without performing surgery. X rays located and identified tumors and other masses. This allowed surgeons to perform better operations. For example,

by using an X ray, a physician could know which part of the lung had the tumor. Rather than opening up both lungs and endangering the patient, now a surgeon could operate only on the affected lung.

Today, X rays are still a very important tool in diagnosing cancers like lung cancer. More recent

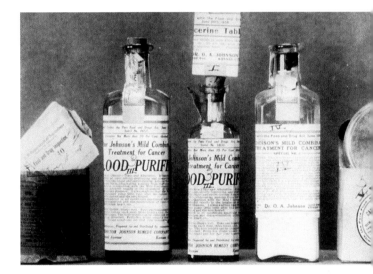

Through the years, many people tried to trick others into buying special medicine that could cure cancer. These tonics and pills did not work and sometimes caused even more sickness.

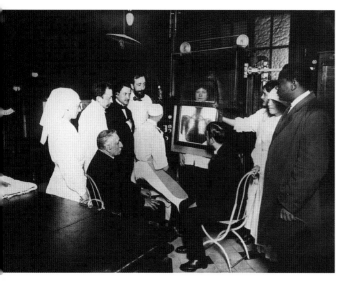

A group of medical professionals examine an X-ray photograph taken by an early X-ray machine.

radiation discoveries were used to create machines that delivered specific amounts of radiation to kill cancerous cells. Radiation can kill cancer cells, but it can also harm healthy cells. Early versions of radiation therapy were often dangerous for patients and the health professionals who used the equipment.

Radiation therapy is still common today, though it is much safer than in years past.

As in earlier centuries, the nineteenth and twentieth centuries yielded progress in medical procedures. Newer surgical tools were used to remove cancerous growths. These new tools caused less damage to a patient's healthy tissues. Physicians began to use **lasers** and other high-tech instruments to destroy tumors. Chemical experimentation resulted in medicine that targeted cancerous cells.

Through the 1900s, the public became more aware of the seriousness of cancer. In 1937, the National Cancer Institute was formed. The institute's mission was to further cancer research in hopes of someday finding a cure. Scientists in laboratories across the country worked together to advance cancer research.

The public started to become aware of cancer issues. More people learned about cancer-causing agents and cancer treatments. In the 1930s, a link between smoking and lung cancer was suggested. However, it was not until decades later that the majority of the public believed this theory.

MOLECULAR BIOLOGY, GENETICS, AND THE FUTURE

In the twentieth and twenty-first centuries, great steps were made to further understand how cells work. New technology allowed scientists to see the tiny structures that make up cells. They could then develop theories on cell function. By understanding how cells

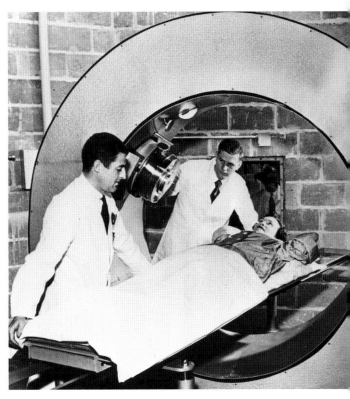

In the 1950s, the "Cobalt bomb" was a radiation therapy used to treat cancer. The therapy involved beaming rays of cobalt, a natural element, into a cancer patient's body.

Secondhand Smoke

....

In the 1970s, a young Greek doctor set out on a quest to convince his wife to quit smoking. He constructed a study to follow 189 women who never smoked. Some lived with smokers and others did not. Results of his study revealed that smokers' wives were twice as likely to develop lung cancer as the wives of non-smokers. After hearing the doctor's findings, his wife quit. The doctor published his findings in 1981.

About the same time, a larger study from Japan made similar claims. Americans took more notice of problems caused by secondhand smoke. By 1993, the United States Environmental Protection Agency (EPA) announced that secondhand smoke was in the same category as other known deadly cancer-causing agents.

worked, scientists could try to find out why some cells stopped working properly, leading to illness. By understanding cancer cells, scientists were also better able to develop medicine and other forms of treatment.

Scientists also gained an understanding of genetics, which is the study of heredity (the passing of genes from parent to child) and variation in organisms. Researchers continue to try to understand why some cells are able to fight cancer and how cells change to become cancerous. Many hope to develop treatments or a cure from genetic research. Perhaps scientists could find a way to change cells so they can be permanently cancer free.

A scientist uses a special microscope to work on cell experiments. Many scientists are trying to find ways to control and change cells to cure and prevent cancer.

Whether the progress deals with improvements in surgery, technology, or genetic research, scientists continue to work toward finding treatments and a possible cure for cancer. But the scientists of today owe their success to the scientists of years past. Without those successes and failures, present-day scientists would not be where they are today.

4

DIAGNOSING, TREATING, AND COPING WITH LUNG CANCER

DIAGNOSING LUNG CANCER

Doctors use a combination of tools to screen for lung cancer. Screening begins with a regular medical exam. During the exam, the doctor asks questions about the patient's general health and if there is a family history of cancer. Doctors will want to know if the patient is a smoker, lives with a smoker, or is exposed to substances that could increase the risk of developing lung cancer.

The patient may be asked to breathe into tubes connected to a machine. These breathing tests measure how well the lungs work. The machine reports how much oxygen the lungs can hold. Depending on the results of the test, more tests might be needed.

A laboratory in New Jersey recently developed a breathalyzer machine that can test for certain types of cancer. Though it is still being tested, many researchers believe that the breathalyzer can analyze a person's breath and detect chemicals that indicate cancer.

Sputum Cytology

One common test for cancer involves looking at fluid from the lungs. The fluid being tested is the mucus, or sputum, from airway linings in parts of the lungs. A scientist looks at the cells of lung fluid under a microscope. The test is called sputum cytology. (Cytology is the study of cells.) The microscope helps the doctor see if the cells look healthy or cancerous. Doctors check the cells for size, shape, and number.

Some scientists believe that abnormal cells might not necessarily indicate cancer but can be a sign that a patient might develop cancer later.

Sputum cytology may give false results of cancer. It is also possible that in some people, lung cancer will not be detected from this test. Some types of cancer may not shed cells that look abnormal. And abnormal cells can also be a sign of other diseases, not necessarily lung cancer. If this is the case, testing mucus samples works as a backup to confirm lung cancer results found by other forms of testing.

X Rays, CT Scans, and PET Scans

X Rays. Using X rays is one way that a health professional can look inside a body. Performing a chest X ray is the most common method for finding problems in the chest. An X ray can usually show a tumor, fluid in the lungs, or an abnormal shape of the lobes of the lungs. By looking closely at X rays, radiologists (doctors who perform and examine special tests such as X rays) can find clues about changes in the lungs that can result from cancer or infections.

Sometimes, X rays show shadows that may or may not be cancer. Most doctors view an X ray as a first screening. They then order other types of tests to confirm the cancer diagnosis.

CT Scans. In recent years, several different imaging tests have become popular. The most promising tool to detect lung cancer is a computed tomography scan or a CT scan. (CT scans are also called CAT scans, for computed axial tomography.) This scan produces images of cross-sections, or slices, of the chest.

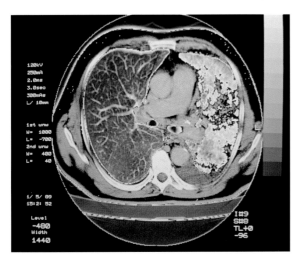

A CT scan of part of the lungs of a 56-year-old man shows healthy lung tissue (left) and cancerous tissue (right).

What Are the Symptoms of Lung Cancer?

Diagnosing lung cancer can be tricky because it sometimes takes years for lung cancer symptoms to show. Some people do not notice symptoms until the cancer has already progressed a few stages. This is why most cases show up in adults over forty years old. Few cases involve people younger than forty, but these cases sometimes do occur.

Another problem is that many symptoms of lung disease are the same as symptoms of other illnesses, such as a cold, the flu, or pneumonia. Because these symptoms may indicate an illness other than lung cancer, it is important for everybody to have regular check ups with their doctors.

Symptoms of lung cancer may include
• A constant cough
• A raspy voice
• Shortness of breath or difficulty breathing
• Noisy breathing
• Frequent colds and flu
• Increased throat mucus
• Chest pain
• A loss of appetite and unplanned weight loss
• Coughing up blood
• Unexplained fever
• Swelling in the face or neck

In order to perform a PET scan, a patient must pass through a large tubelike structure that scans the body.

The pictures show features of the tumor and give some idea if the cancer has spread beyond the lungs. Experts believe a CT scan is one of the best ways to look for lung cancer because it can show more detail than regular X rays. This allows doctors to find smaller tumors earlier. Removing a tumor before it has a chance to grow and spread can increase a patient's chance of survival.

PET Scans. Another imaging test is the positron emission tomography (PET). Unlike X rays or CT scans, PET scans do not only show how cells look but also how they work. Before performing a PET scan, doctors inject a sugary liquid into the patient's body. A PET scan allows a doctor to see how quickly the cells are using the sugars. Cancer cells use sugars faster than healthy cells. By looking at the scans, doctors can assume that the cells using sugar quicker are most likely cancer cells.

Testing Tumor Cells

Scans are good for learning about tumors. But doctors need solid proof that cancer cells exist before treatment can begin. The only way to prove whether or not tissue has cancer is to take a sample for study. This is called a **biopsy**.

To obtain sample cells, doctors sometimes cut into the lung area. Depending upon the location of the tumor, a doctor may also get a lung cell sample by using a hollow needle. The needle (attached to a **syringe**) is guided through the chest to the tumor with help from a scan. Sample cells from the tumor are then drawn through the needle into the syringe. Doctors can examine the cells under a microscope.

Another method for closely examining lung cells is through endoscopy. With endoscopy, a tiny camera on the end of a tube is threaded into the lung. The tube is usually inserted through the nose, mouth, or a small incision (cut) in the chest. If the camera

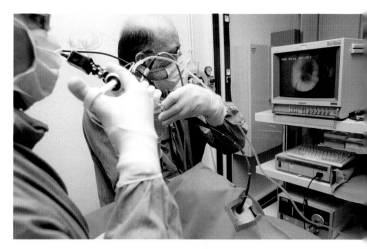

A bronchoscope (a special type of endoscope) is inserted into the lungs to look for signs of cancer.

finds a growth, a piece is removed and checked under the microscope.

The Stages of Lung Cancer

In order to track and describe the progression of a person's cancer, many health professionals use a list of cancer stages for small cell and non-small cell lung cancer. Here is one version of the list of stages determined by the U.S. Food and Drug Administration (FDA):

Small Cell Lung Cancer

THE LIMITED STAGE: Tumors are usually only found in one lung and in the lymph nodes on the same side of the chest.
THE EXTENSIVE STAGE: The cancer has spread to the other lung and to lymph nodes on the other side of the chest.

Non-Small Cell Lung Cancer

OCCULT STAGE: Doctors cannot yet find tumors in the lungs, but a patient's saliva indicates that cancer is present.
STAGE 0: The cancer is found only in a few layers of lung cells. It has not spread to the lung's outermost lining.
STAGE I: The tumor is only in the lung. The tissue around the tumor is still normal and cancer free.

STAGE II: Cancer cells have spread to the lymph nodes near the tumor.

STAGE III: Cancer cells have spread to the chest wall, or to the diaphragm, or to the lymph nodes in the area between the two lungs, or to the lymph nodes in the neck or both sides of the chest.

STAGE IIIA: The cancer is a single tumor or a single mass. The tumor can be removed by surgery.

STAGE IIIB: Because the cancer has spread too much and there are too many tumors, surgery is no longer an option. Chemotherapy and radiation treatments may be tried.

STAGE IV: This is the most advanced stage. The cancer cells have spread to other parts of the body.

TREATMENT

Different tests show an oncologist the stage of the cancer. This allows the doctor to plan a course of treatment. Treatments for lower stages of cancer tend to be less forceful. As the cancer reaches later stages, the treatments might be stronger. The type and frequency of the treatment depends upon the stage of cancer.

Surgery

During surgery to remove cancer tissue, either part of the lung or an entire lobe may be removed. Recovery can be slow and painful, and it often takes weeks or months to heal. Cutting into the lungs may also damage some healthy tissues.

Studies have shown that patients recover faster if doctors use lasers rather than traditional cutting tools, such as **scalpels**. In laser surgery, an instrument is inserted into the airway near the tumor. A strong laser beam at the end of the instrument shines on the tumor, burning and destroying the cancer cells. Doctors also recommend surgery in late-stage cancer to relieve pain or discomfort from a tumor lodged in a troublesome place.

The type of surgery depends on the size and location of the tumor. Sometimes a doctor cannot use a laser to destroy a tumor. But both types of surgery should completely remove cancer that is localized in one area and has not spread.

Radiation Therapy

Radiation therapy uses high doses of radiation to shrink or kill cancer cells. Radiation can be the main treatment for people unable to undergo surgery. For others, radiation is used to remove cancerous growths that cannot be reached through surgery. Some oncologists prescribe radiation therapy in addition to surgery and other forms of treatment.

There are two ways to undergo radiation therapy. One way involves using a machine that directs a radiated beam toward the cancer. Another process uses radioactive material in the form of a capsule. This radioactive capsule is inserted into the body and placed near the tumor. As the capsule breaks down, radiation is released, killing the cancer cells.

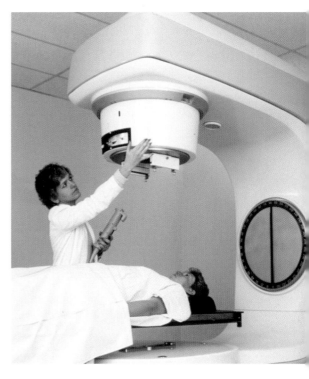

This patient is undergoing radiation therapy to treat her cancer.

Oncologists carefully calculate the amount of radiation to use. This prevents damage to healthy cells. Side effects of radiation therapy may include **nausea**, loss of appetite, tiredness (fatigue), or skin irritation near the radiation site. Many oncologists prescribe pain relievers to ease the pain caused by the treatment.

Chemotherapy

Chemotherapy involves taking medications (chemicals) that kill cancer cells. Chemotherapy can be given by mouth in pill form or put into the bloodstream through injection or patches.

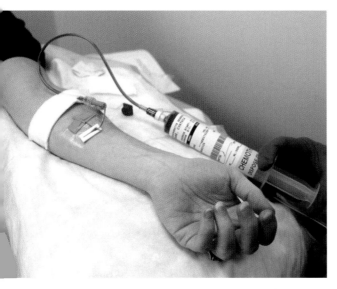

A cancer patient undergoes chemotherapy. The medication is injected directly into her bloodstream.

Once in the bloodstream, the chemicals travel throughout the body, killing cancer that has spread into different parts.

Chemotherapy tends to be very effective but has some serious side effects. The main problem with chemotherapy involves the strength of the chemicals. In order to kill cancer cells, the chemicals need to be really strong. But the chemicals can also kill healthy cells as well. When this happens, a patient might experience loss of appetite, nausea, or fatigue.

Because cells, such as taste buds, can be affected by chemotherapy, a cancer patient undergoing treatment may lose the sense of taste. Cuts, bruises, or other wounds may also take longer to heal because of chemotherapy. Medication is often given to relieve pain, to stimulate a person's appetite, or to prevent infection of slow-healing wounds.

Unfortunately, the side effects of cancer treatments can take a very serious toll on cancer patients. Because of the fatigue and the pain, some give up hope and no longer care about getting better. A growing number of people with severe lung cancer refuse treatment. They would rather deal with the pain lung cancer causes rather than suffer from the side effects of the treatment.

It is important to remember that lung cancer is often deadly, and in many cases, treatment is not an option. If lung cancer has spread too much and organ systems are failing, no amount of treatment can help these people recover. At this stage, many doctors offer emotional support and suggest making the patients as comfortable as possible.

COPING WITH LUNG CANCER

People who hear that they have lung cancer often struggle with a range of feelings. Many become overwhelmed with fear, sadness, and anger. Even when treatment goes well and the cancer looks to have disappeared (which is called remission), cancer survivors must deal with the constant worry of cancer returning. There are different ways to help people who have lung cancer cope better with the difficulties of having and treating the disease.

Pain Management

Lung cancer in its later stages can be a very painful disease. The cancer itself can cause great discomfort, but so can treatments. Many doctors prescribe medication to ease a patient's pain. Patients worry, however, that these drugs may make them too sleepy or unaware of what is going on around them. Some are even concerned about becoming addicted to pain medication.

Many cancer patients find that massage, acupressure, or acupuncture can help with managing pain management. Massage and acupressure work to ease tense or sore muscles and improve blood flow, hopefully relieving some of the pain. Acupuncture involves inserting very slender needles into the skin. These needles target specific areas on the body that professionals believe will ease nausea and pain. Acupuncture should be performed only by a trained professional who uses clean supplies.

Physical Well-Being

For the most part, the growth of the cancer is beyond the control of the cancer patient. There are, however, things that a person can still control. Many cancer patients find that trying to maintain good physical health helps during cancer treatments.

Though cancer patients may lose their appetite and sense of taste, they should try to maintain a healthful, balanced diet. The body still needs nutrients to keep it running. Eating

Alternative Therapies

....

Many patients choose to pursue alternative therapies, which are treatments that are outside standard medicine. Some of these therapies have been tested in other countries, but not approved by the FDA or the American Medical Association (AMA) in the United States. In many cases, most oncologists will not recommend these treatments in the place of surgery, radiation therapy, or chemotherapy.

Sometimes these alternative therapies are used to ease the discomfort from the cancer and its traditional medical treatments. Alternative therapies are also used by patients who cannot be treated through traditional measures or who have undergone surgery, radiation, or chemotherapy with little success. Whatever the reason, before undergoing alternative therapies, cancer patients should talk to their doctor.

Diet. Several diets claim to rid a person of poisons that collect in the body and cause disease. These diets are usually strict vegetarian diets that allow only organic foods, those free of preservatives and other chemicals, and prohibit dairy products and red meats. But doctors worry that limited and unproven diets weaken bodies that need food for energy. Eating organic fruits, vegetables, and grains helps the body fight disease, but a person's diet should be well-rounded and include all the basic food groups.

Vitamins and Herbs. Some people outside the medical community believe that large doses of certain vitamins, herbs, or other substances help the body's immune system, which helps it fight off disease and infections. Several vitamins and herbs are being tested for their ability to keep damaged cells from multiplying. Early studies suggest that forms of vitamin A might decrease cancer cells or stop them from dividing and multiplying. Other studies investigate how well vitamin E and selenium protect body cells against damage. But these studies are not conclusive. Having a lot of these vitamins and minerals might protect against lung cancer, but too much can be dangerous.

fruits, vegetables, meats, and other nutrient-rich foods can help. A **nutritious** diet can also help to maintain a person's energy levels. With higher energy levels, a cancer patient might feel less tired or depressed.

Some cancer patients continue to perform some sort of exercise routine even during treatments. However, it is important for a patient to talk to his or her doctor about the right type and amount of exercise. Depending upon the severity of the cancer, a patient may not be able to engage in heavy exercise. Even taking short walks or stretching can help. Keeping the muscles active can help fight fatigue and some pain.

Doctors recommend deep breathing as one way to ease muscle pain. Another approach is to tighten each muscle and then think hard about letting it rest, releasing it slowly. Focusing on healthy muscles not only loosens stiff muscles but also lessens thoughts of discomfort elsewhere. Many cancer patients also find that gentle stretching or yoga helps. Some claim that yoga gently exercises their muscles while also helping them to relax.

Support Groups

People with lung cancer face many challenges. Sometimes, just talking about feelings helps patients and their families cope better. Many patients and families find comfort in support groups. These groups are made up of people who have cancer or have a loved one with cancer. Support groups may also include people who had cancer, but are now cancer free, and people who lost loved ones to cancer. Sometimes these groups include medical professionals who are trained to help people cope with the stress, pain, and grief that cancer brings.

Group members can share their feelings, talk about recent discoveries, and give and receive advice on how to keep life as normal as possible while dealing with cancer. Individuals with cancer can join a group on their own or with family members. Family members and friends of any age can locate a separate group to help them learn the best way to support a loved one with cancer. Hospitals, cancer centers, and doctors' offices often have information about local support groups.

There is no cure for lung cancer, though scientists are working toward finding better treatments and hopefully a cure. The best thing anyone dealing with the disease can do is to stay informed. Understanding lung cancer is the best way to fight it.

GLOSSARY

abnormal—Not normal.

addicted—To have a strong need for something. People become addicted to substances such as tobacco, drugs, or alcohol.

benign—Harmless.

biopsy—The removal and examination of cells located inside the body.

carcinogens—Substances that can cause cancer.

chemotherapy—A cancer treatment which uses strong medication to kill cancer cells.

cilia—Hairlike structures that trap dirt particles and some other harmful substances.

defect—A flaw or weakness. If something has defects it is defective.

diagnosis—The act of determining what is making a person sick.

genetics—The study of heredity (receiving biological traits from parents) and variation in organisms.

laser—A device that creates a strong beam of light.

malignant—Harmful and cancer-causing.

metastasis—The spread of cancerous cells.

microscope—An instrument used to look at things that are too small to be seen by the human eye.

mucus—Sticky fluid that coats different parts inside the body.

nausea—Sick feelings in a person's stomach.

nerves—Bundles of fibers that carry and send messages to and from the brain and other parts of the body. Nerves allow a person to feel or sense things and move body parts.

nutritious—To be useful to and healthy for the body.

oncogenes—Genes that cause cancer.

radiation—Energy that is given off in waves, particles, or rays. Radiation therapy is used to kill cancer cells.

respiratory system—The set of body parts that move air into and out of the body.

scalpel—A sharp instrument used to cut things.

secondhand smoke—Smoke that comes from the end of a burning tobacco product and smoke that a smoker exhales. A person standing next to a smoker will most likely inhale the smoker's secondhand smoke.

symptoms—Signs that indicate the presence of a disease or illness.

syringe—A hollow device used to withdraw or inject something. Syringes can be used to draw blood or inject medicine.

tumors—Groups of fast-growing cells.

wheeze—To make noisy, whistling sounds while breathing.

FIND OUT MORE

Organizations

Alliance for Lung Cancer Advocacy, Support, and Education (ALCASE)

500 West 8th Street, Suite 240

Vancouver, WA 98660

1-800-298-2436

www.alcase.org

American Lung Association

61 Broadway, 6th Floor

New York, NY 10006

1-800-LUNG-USA (800-586-4872)

www.lungusa.org

National Cancer Institute

NCI Public Inquiries Office

6116 Executive Boulevard

Room 3036A

Bethesda, MD 20892-8322

1-800-4-CANCER (1-800-422-6237)

www.cancer.gov

Books

Gold, John Coopersmith. *Cancer*. Berkeley Heights, NJ: Enslow, 2001.

Hirschfelder, Arlene. *Kick Butts-A Kid's Action Guide to a Tobacco-Free America*. Parsippany, NJ: Silver Burdett Press, 1998.

Massari, Francesca. *Everything You Need to Know About Cancer*. New York: Rosen Publishing Group, 2000.

Sanders, Pete and Steve Myers. *Smoking*. Brookfield, CT: Copper Beech Books, 1996.

Scott, Walter. *Lung Cancer: A Guide to Diagnosis and Treatment*. Omaha, NE: Addicus Books, 2000.

Silverstein, Alvin, Virginia Silverstein, and Laura Silverstein Nunn. *Smoking*. Danbury, CT: Franklin Watts, 2003.

Web Sites

CancerBACUP
http://www.cancerbacup.org.uk/Cancertype/Lung

It's Time to Focus on Lung Cancer
http://www.lungcancer.org

Kids Against Tobacco Smoke
(Roy Castle Lung Cancer Foundation)
http://www.roycastle.org/kats/intro.htm

Learn About Cancer (American Cancer Society)
http://www.cancer.org/docroot/LRN/LRN_0.asp

Lung Cancer (National Cancer Institute)
http://www.nci.nih.gov/cancerinfo/types/lung

Lung Cancer Online
http://www.lungcanceronline.org

INDEX

Page numbers for illustrations are in **boldface**

air pollutants, 26, 30, **31**
airways, 11, 14, 20
alternative therapies, 55
alveoli, 11–12, **11, 12**, 13, **13**, 20
appetite, 14, 41–42
asbestos, 28–30, **28, 29**
asbestosis, 29

biopsy, 47,
blood, 11–12, 14, 15, 17, 20
   vessels, 11–12, **12**
bloodstream, 14,
breathalyzer, 43, **43**
breathing, 6, 10–12, 29
bronchi, 11, **11**, 12, 18
bronchioles, 11, **11**

cancer,
   breast, 8
   history of, 32–41, **33, 34, 35, 36, 37, 38, 39, 41**
   stomach, 8
   types of, 8–9
capillaries, 11–12, **12**
carbon dioxide, 12
carcinogens, 20–31
   See also air pollutants, asbestos, radon, smoking
carcinoma, 34
cell, 8, 13, 26
   cancer, 8, 9, **9**, 13, **13**, 15, **15**, 18–20, **18, 19**, 22, 39, 43–44
      See also non-small cell lung cancer, small cell lung cancer
   damage, 13, 21, 22
   death, 8, 13, 20
   defects, 8
   growth, 8, 23
   multiplication, 8

chemotherapy, 7, 51–53, **52**
cilia, 13,
colds, 6, 14
coughing, 6, 14
CT scans (CAT scans), 44, 45–46 **45**

diet, 7, 55, 56

endoscopy, 47–48, **47**
exercise, 56

fever, 6
flu, 6, 14

genes, 25–26
   See also oncogenes
genetics, 23, 25–26, 39, 40

heart, 10,
   disease, 22
heredity, 25, 26
Hippocrates, 32, 34, **34**

lasers, 38
leukemia, 10
lobes, 10–11, **11**
lung cancer
   diagnosis, 42–48, **43, 45, 46, 47**
   family medical history, 20
   in men, 22
   in women, 22
   stages of, 48–49
   symptoms, 6–7, 10, 13, 45
   treatment, 10, 20, 23, 49–53
      side effects, 52–53
         See also alternative therapies, chemotherapy, radiation, surgery
   types of, 18–20, **18, 19**

lungs, 7, **11, 14**, 16, **16**, 24, **24**
   function, 10–12, 13, 29
   structure, 10–12
lymph nodes, 17, **17**

lymphatic
  system, 17, **17**, 35
  vessels, 17, **17**

metastasis, 7, 16, **16**, 17, 48–49
  See also lymphatic
microscope, 18, 34, 43
mouth, 11, **11**, 12, 47
mucus, 13, 14

nerves, 15
non–small cell lung cancer, 18–20, **19**, 48
nose, 11, **11**, 12, 47
nutrients, 13

oat cell cancer, *See* small cell lung cancer
oncogenes, 26
  See also genes, genetics
oncologist, 7
organs, 8, 16
oxygen, 10, 12, 13, 220

pain, 6, 7, 15, 16, 51, 52
  management, 53–54
PET scans, 44, 46, **46**
pleura, 10–11

radiation, 37, 38
  treatments, 7, 38, 39, **39**, 50–51, **51**
radon, 26–28

testing, 27, **27**
research, 39–41, **41**
respiratory system, 10–11, 12, **11**, **12**, **13**

secondhand smoke, 23, 25, 26, 40
small cell lung cancer, 18–19, **18**, 48
smoking, 6, 7, 19, 20–25, **21**, **24**, 26
sneezing, 14
sputum cytology, 43–44
statistics, 22, 23, 26, 27, 30
support, 7, 57
surgery, 7, 36, **36**, 50

tobacco, 20–22, **21**, 23
  See also smoking
trachea, 11, **11**
tumor, 10, 12, 13, **13**, 14, **14**, 15, 16, **16**,
  18–20, 24, **24**, 26, 32, 36, 44, 47, 47, 48–
  49, 50, 51
    benign, 10, 32
    malignant, 10, 32

weight loss, 15
wheezing, 6
white blood cells, 17

X ray, 10, 37, 38, **38**, 44

ABOUT THE AUTHOR

Marlene Targ Brill writes about many topics, from history and biographies to sports and world peace. Her favorite topics involve ways to help people become healthier. When she was growing up, Marlene loved learning about the body. She came from a family of pharmacists who prepared and sold medicine to make people feel better. At one time, she wanted to be a nurse. Instead, she became a teacher of children who had special needs. Now she writes about special needs and other health topics for children and adults. She lives near Chicago with her husband, Richard, and daughter, Alison.